100

MIGRATION IN THE SEA

All animals migrate. A migration is any planned journey from one place to another. This book describes some interesting and extraordinary migrations ranging from a few yards to several thousand miles.

MIGRATION IN THE SEA

Liz Oram

and

R. Robin Baker

Department of Environmental Biology
University of Manchester

STECK-VAUGHN
LIBRARY
A Division of Steck-Vaughn Company
Austin, Texas

Library of Congress Cataloging-in-Publication Data

Oram, Liz, 1964–
Migrations in the sea / Liz Oram and R. Robin Baker.
p.   cm.—(Migrations)
Includes index.

Summary: Describes the migration patterns of such
marine animals as turtles, whales, salmon, anemones,
barnacles, crabs, and sea lions.

ISBN 0-8114-2928-8
1. Marine fauna—Migration—Juvenile literature.
[1. Marine animals—Migration.   2. Marine animals—
Habits and behavior.]   I. Baker, Robin, 1944–
II. Title.   III. Series: Oram, Liz, 1964–   Migrations.
QL122.2.073   1991   91-12765
591.52′5—dc20   CIP AC

Cover: *Sea lions at a Galapagos*
Islands breeding ground.

Typeset by Multifacit Graphics, Keyport, NJ
Printed in Hong Kong
Bound in the United States by Lake Book, Melrose Park, IL

1 2 3 4 5 6 7 8 9 0 HK 96 95 94 93 92

Contents

Introduction

Every year thousands of whales set off on journeys that are often as long as 12,000 miles. They start in the cold, northern and southern oceans and end in the warmer seas near the Equator.

Whales are not the only sea animals that make journeys. Many

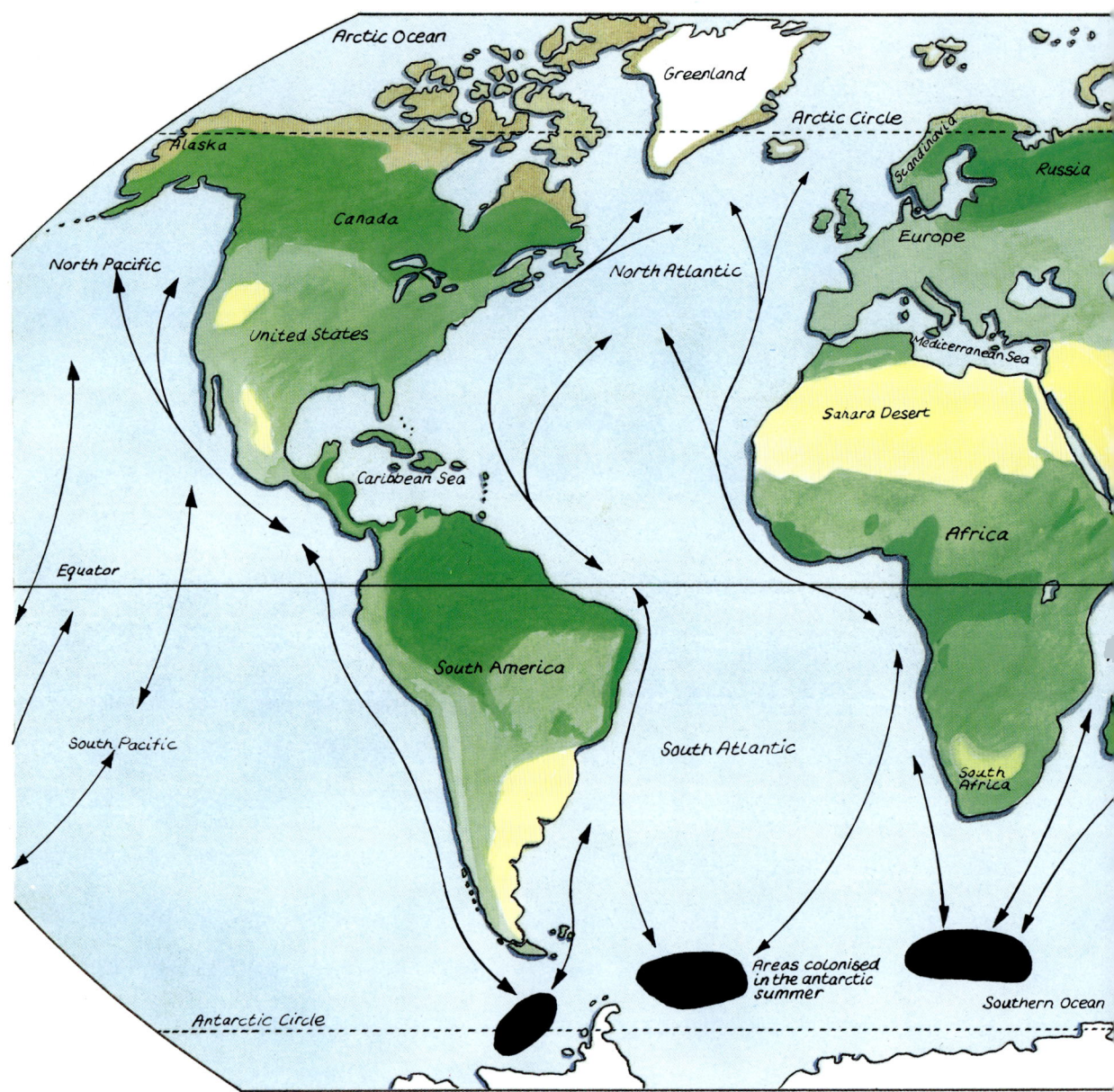

animals, some of them no bigger than a pinhead, regularly make journeys of hundreds of miles. In fact, the sea is full of animals making journeys. Some are just below the waves, others are far beneath the surface. Some are on their way to the shore. Others, like the whales, are heading for different waters. Some, like the salmon, are on their way to inland rivers.

Animals that make journeys are called "migrants." The journeys they make are called "migrations." Sea animals migrate in many different ways. Tuna fish, for example, migrate in large groups called "schools." When schools of tuna pass through shallow waters, the surface of the sea swells with the movement of these shiny, gliding fish. Other sea animals, like the turtle, migrate thousands of miles on their own. Not all sea animals migrate by swimming, though. There is a type of lobster that migrates by walking in a long procession along the ocean floor.

It is not easy to watch sea animals migrating. Some migrants, such as whales, have to come up to the surface every so often to breathe. We can at least catch a glimpse of them as they emerge briefly through the waves. We can see other migrants, like the turtle, as they get near the shore. Only people who have been trained to dive deep down into the oceans are able to see more.

For many of us, this makes migration in the sea even more interesting and wonderful than the migrations of mammals, birds, and insects on land and in the air.

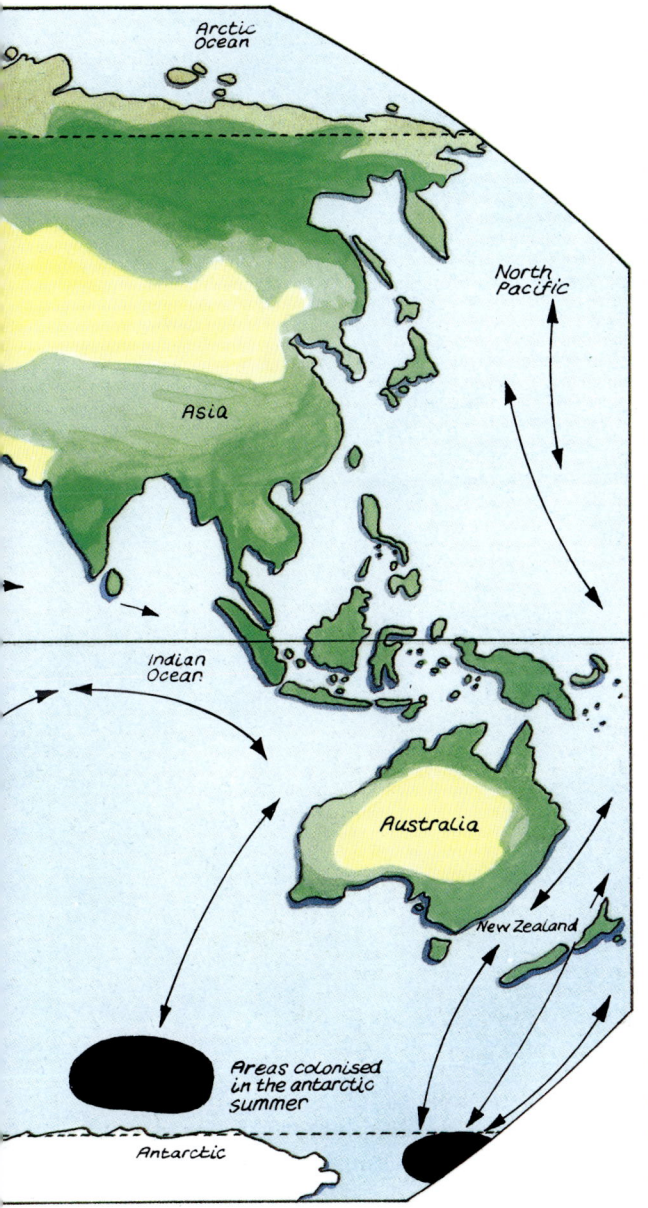

This map shows the migration routes of the humpback whale. Humpbacks are found in all oceans. They migrate to polar waters in summer to feed, and back to tropical waters in winter.

The blue whale is the largest creature that has ever lived. Only a small part of it shows here, where it has risen to the surface to breathe.

1 Animals on the Rocky Shore

A rocky shore is one of the most exciting places to explore. Perhaps you can remember clambering over rocks and peering into tide pools on a visit to the coast. Did you notice that the rocks were often covered with tiny animals? Some of them look just like shells, others feel slimy to the touch. The tide pools are also

Ebb tide in Monterey Bay, California. Thousands of tiny creatures will now seek a hiding place until the next tide.

teeming with life. Perhaps you saw a tiny fish dart across a pool. Besides fish, in some tide pools there are animals that look just like flowers. These are called "sea anemones."

In this chapter we are going to look at all these different animals. They all have a fixed home, and most of them make only tiny migrations in order to find food. Some, like the barnacle, cannot move at all.

Tide pools come in all shapes and

sizes. Some are no bigger than puddles. Others can be several yards across. Water collects to form tide pools whenever the rock is shaped like a basin or a saucer. This water has been left behind from the last time the rocks were covered by the tide. When the tide is in, all the tide pools are under water. As the tide goes out the rocks are uncovered, but seawater stays in every hollow to form tide pools.

This tide pool is home to the creatures you see here. They will migrate between tides, but will always return.

Most of the creatures in tide pools were not left behind by the tide. The pool is their home and they will still be there after the next tide. During high tides, other creatures in the pool migrate.

Sea Anemones, Periwinkles, Blennies, and Gobies

These are the odd-sounding names of just a few of the animals that live in tide pools. Sea anemones are beautiful, strange animals that look just like flowers. Brightly colored in reds, greens, and blues, they are easy

These beautiful sea anemones look like plants, but they are just as much animals as the fish swimming above them.

to spot and exciting to find. Sea anemones do not travel very far. Most of the time they are anchored to a rock. They feed on tiny animals that swim too close, catching their victims with their long, slender tentacles.

A periwinkle is a type of snail. Unlike most of the snails that live on land, periwinkle shells come in lots of pretty colors. They can be yellow, white, and sometimes even pink.

Some tide pools contain fish. In most parts of the world these fish are called blennies or gobies. Some blennies or gobies can grow to a length of eight inches or more. When the tide goes out all of these fish hide in their tide pools. They lie quietly under pieces of seaweed, but if the seaweed is disturbed they dart out across the pool.

When the tide comes in, the tide pool joins with the sea. The periwinkles crawl out of their pools and roam around on the surrounding rocks, looking for food. Periwinkles have tongues shaped like nail files. They use them to scrape off the tiny plants that grow on the surface of the rocks. Periwinkles can tell when the tide is going to go out again. They always make sure they are back in their tide pools before the falling tide

High tide level

Low tide level

leaves them stranded on the dry rocks.

The blennies and gobies also come out of the tide pools when the tide is in. They may swim many yards away to find food. Like the periwinkles, though, they always make sure they are back home before the tide falls.

Barnacles

If you live near a coast you might have noticed the gray-colored, sharp shells that cluster on many of the rocks. Have you ever tried to pull any of them off? If you have, you know that they are stuck fast. This is because there is an animal living inside the shell.

This animal is the barnacle. The barnacle lives inside its shell in much the same way a turtle does. It produces a sticky substance that glues the shell to the rock or whatever else it attaches itself to.

When the tide is high it covers the rocks. When the tide goes down, water is left in the hollows of the rocks, forming tide pools.

Barnacles are found on rocky shores all over the world. Sometimes the rocks are completely covered with them. They can be packed so tightly that smaller barnacles actually sit on top of larger ones. Some barnacle shells are so small they can hardly be seen. Others may be as big as an inch across.

A barnacle is an animal that stands on its head and kicks food into its mouth with its legs! If you look closely at a barnacle shell you will see a slit at the top. When the tide is out this slit is tightly closed. It keeps the barnacle inside from getting too dry. Barnacles die if they become too dry. When the tide comes in the barnacle opens this slit and waves its legs in the water. These legs are very hairy and look a bit like a fan.

12

Barnacles on a South African beach. They cluster so thickly that there can be thousands of them in a square yard.

Floating around in seawater are lots of tiny plants and animals. Some are so small that they can only be seen with a microscope. These tiny plants and animals are called "plankton." The barnacle's legs are just right for trapping plankton. The barnacle sweeps its legs through the water and down toward its mouth. There it sucks the plankton it has caught off its legs. Then it sweeps its legs again through the water to catch some more. When the tide falls the barnacle has to stop feeding. It tucks its legs back into its shell and goes to sleep until the tide comes back in again.

Barnacles stick their shells onto rocks very firmly. Once a barnacle is attached to a rock, it never moves. Surprisingly, though, as you will read later, some barnacles travel hundreds of miles before attaching themselves to rocks, dock piles, or boat keels.

Limpets

This animal is a type of snail. It is dark brown in color, and feels slimy to the touch. Limpets are found on rocky beaches all over the world. Sometimes they have barnacles growing on their shells. Unlike barnacles, though, which are stuck to the rocks and cannot move, limpets can walk around whenever they want to. Just like land snails, they have one big, flat foot. When the tide is in they use that foot to glide over the rocks.

However, when the tide is out, the limpet has to hold onto its rock very tightly. Large birds like gulls like to eat limpets. They pull the limpet from the rock, turn the shell upside down, and eat the animal underneath. The gull has to work very hard, though, to pull the limpet off its rock. Each limpet has a special

Over several years, limpets grind homes out of the rock. Each of these shallow pits belongs to one particular limpet.

place on the rock where it sleeps when the tide is out. Gradually, over months, the limpet grinds down the surface of the rock to make a small dent. This dent fits the limpet's shell exactly. It is called the limpet's "depression." The limpet lives in its depression, making it very difficult for the gull to get a grip.

When the tide is in and the limpet is covered with water, it leaves its home depression and wanders off to find food. Just like the periwinkle, it has a tongue shaped like a nail file. The limpet uses its tongue to scrape food off the rocks. While it is feeding, the limpet may travel as far as a yard from its home. It is very important, however, that the limpet

You can see where this limpet fed, by the track it left behind. But now the tide is out and the limpet is back in its home.

gets home before the tide goes down. As soon as the rocks are exposed, birds start looking for the few unlucky limpets that have not gotten home in time.

A limpet can tell when the tide starts to go down. When the tide does fall, the limpet begins to feel its way back over the rock, just like you would if you were blindfolded. A limpet learns how every part of its rock feels. It also learns how different parts of its rock smells. It guides itself home by feeling and smelling the rock's surface.

2 Moving to a New Home

Sometimes, the rocky shore becomes a difficult place in which to live. In summer, when the sun shines for long periods, the rocks and sand can get very hot. You may have noticed this yourself. People often burn their feet when the sand is that hot. Sometimes the water in tide pools becomes too hot for the fish, or it may even dry up completely. In winter the rocks get very cold and are sometimes covered with ice. In stormy weather waves crash onto the rocks, and some of the animals in the pools may get battered around or swept out.

Animals that live on the rocky shore soon realize if they have chosen a bad place to live. In this chapter, we shall see what they do when their homes become too uncomfortable for them.

Barnacles are "glued" to the rock. They cannot move. If a barnacle's rock becomes unbearably hot or cold, or if the waves crash too hard, it will eventually die.

Limpets do not like having to leave their homes. It often takes a limpet several years to grind out its home depression. If the animal moves it will have to start grinding out a new one. It will also have to learn how to find its way home to a different place. A homeless limpet is likely to be attacked by birds as it searches for a new home.

However, limpets are crafty animals. They try to make moving to a new home as easy for themselves as possible. Often they will try to steal another limpet's home depression. The homeless limpet moves slowly onto the other limpet's rock. Then, usually when this other limpet is out feeding, it launches an attack. Instead of trying to race back to its depression, the other limpet usually stays and fights.

Fighting for a New Home

A limpet fight is strange to watch. Limpets fight by butting each other very, very slowly. They look as if they are fighting in slow motion. Each limpet tries to get the edge of its shell under the shell of the other. When this is done, the loser is lifted up high into the air and forced off the rock. Usually, of course, the bigger limpet wins.

When a limpet steals the home of another, the new depression is not a perfect fit. The new limpet has to grind the rock to fit its own shell. However, this is still faster than starting from the beginning.

The tiny goby lives under rocks in tide pools. A goby's memory of its habitat is so good that it can make its way up and down the beach at low tide by jumping from one pool to another, even though it cannot see the next pool.

Tide Pool Fish

In very hot weather many tide pools overheat. The fish that live in them become uncomfortable, so they move to deeper or shadier pools. An overheated blenny or goby moves its home in a spectacular way. It literally jumps from its old tide pool into a new one. Sometimes they jump as far as three to six feet over the bare rocks. They hardly ever make mistakes and land between two pools. This is incredible because a fish cannot see the tide pool it is jumping into. So how does it know which direction to jump or how far to jump?

The answer is that the fish makes preparations. When the tide is in, all the tide pools are underwater. The fish explores all the dips and basins around its home tide pool. It knows where all the neighboring tide pools will be when the tide goes out again. Amazingly, it remembers the direction and distance of all these nearby pools. This is how it knows where to jump.

3 Traveling on the Ocean Currents

Things that float in the water never stay completely still. They are carried along by the ocean currents. If you sit in a small rowboat on the sea and do not row, the boat is carried along by the current. Rowing against the current is hard work. Rowing with the current, however, is much easier. It is almost like having a free ride. Some currents go in more or less straight lines for thousands of miles. Others go around in enormous circles thousands of miles across. Some currents just go around and around in small bays, while others travel a few miles along coasts before becoming very weak.

In this chapter we will look at a few animals that use the ocean currents to help them migrate either short or long distances.

Barnacles

Some barnacles might travel hundreds of miles before glueing themselves to rocks. A newborn barnacle is called a barnacle "larva." A barnacle larva is very tiny and has no shell, but it can swim. It is born when the tide is in and the parent barnacle is covered with water. This tiny animal swims around in the

water and gets carried out to sea by the current. Here, it becomes part of the plankton that we looked at earlier.

The barnacle larva remains as plankton for a few weeks, feeding on

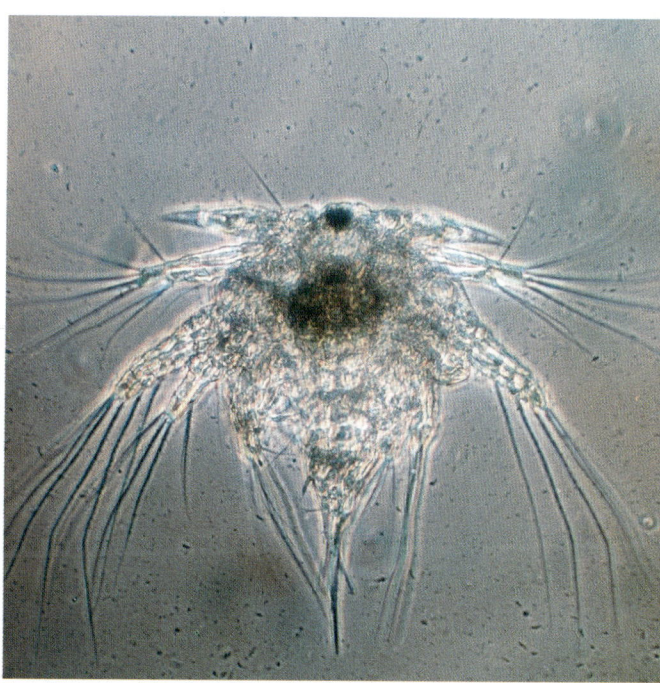

The barnacle larva may migrate hundreds of miles in currents. But when ready to become an adult, it paddles into position over a rock, glues itself into place, and never moves again.

other plankton. If the larva is lucky, the current will eventually carry it to another rocky shore. This new shore may be hundreds of miles from the one where it was born. When it lands on a rock, the larva stands on its head, glues itself to the rock surface, and starts to grow a shell. Soon it looks just like a tiny adult barnacle.

The barnacle larva is not the only type of larva that uses water currents to reach new shores. Crabs, lobsters, sea urchins, and starfish also produce larvae that float along in many of the ocean currents.

Codfish

Codfish live in the Atlantic Ocean, and are very good to eat. Great numbers of cod are caught in massive nets drawn along through the sea. For most of their lives, cod swim among the plankton and are carried along by the currents. When they are young and small they feed on the tiny animals that live in the plankton. Older cod eat other fish, such as herring.

The codfish lays an amazing number of eggs. In one year a single cod can lay as many as 15 million eggs! Only a few of these eggs reach adulthood, though. The eggs float in the water and are carried along in the plankton by the current. Most of them are eaten by all sorts of sea creatures. After a few weeks the eggs

Cod never cease migrating. Young cod change habitat according to size and their ability to avoid predators. Adults move from inshore waters in winter to deeper water in summer. They make long journeys, such as from Newfoundland to Greenland.

hatch into young cod, and are preyed upon by other fish. When they are about six months old, they drop down to the bottom of the sea for a year or so. Here they feed on tiny crabs and prawns. Eventually, when they are fully grown, they swim up to join the older cod again.

Cod spend most of the rest of their lives swimming along in the ocean currents. They are clever enough to

swim in currents that go in the direction in which they want to migrate.

Cod are quite big fish. They can grow to a length of six feet and weigh more than 200 pounds when fully grown. Yet they still find it easier to swim with the ocean currents than against them. However, cod are not the biggest animals that use ocean currents to get an easy ride. The tuna fish may grow to a length of thirteen feet and often weighs as much as 1,000 pounds. Sea turtles may be nearly six feet long and have a very heavy shell. Even these strong animals use the ocean currents to help them migrate. You will find out more about these two animals later on in the book. Even some of the larger sharks use the currents to help them migrate.

4 Moving with the Seasons

Rocky shores are always changing with the seasons. They become hot in summer, cold in winter, and are battered by the tides in spring and fall. We have already seen how some animals migrate if their homes become too uncomfortable. These animals are living dangerously, though. They wait *until* it becomes uncomfortable before moving. Sometimes they wait too long and die before they can migrate.

In this chapter, you will read about animals that do not take this risk.

They move *before* conditions become uncomfortable. They migrate to cooler places to spend the summer, and to warmer places to spend the winter. They also migrate to avoid running out of food. Some of them, like the sea urchins, crabs, and tide pool fish, are quite small and only move up and down the shore.

People fortunate enough to go diving can see marine creatures in their natural habitat. This plantlike creature is in fact a white-tipped feather star, a sea animal.

Others, like sea lions, are much larger and migrate between the shore and the sea.

Sea urchins move on protruding tubefeet with suckers. On taking a grip, the front feet shorten, pulling the urchin forward.

Sea Urchins

Perhaps you have been warned about the various dangers of swimming in the ocean. But has anyone ever warned you about sea urchins? The round-shaped sea urchins are entirely covered with sharp spines, like a porcupine's spines. Some sea urchins grow as large as soccer balls. Others stay quite small, but even the smallest have spines.

The spines are very brittle. If you

accidentally step on a sea urchin, the sharp spines stick into your foot and then break off. They are difficult to remove. It is no use trying to pull them out because they just keep breaking. You just have to wait until the spines finally drop out by themselves. This can take a very long time and be quite painful.

If you look closely at a sea urchin under water, you will see thousands of long, thin, fleshy threads among the spines. Although they look very fragile, these threads are quite strong. They are the animal's arms and legs. The ones underneath the animal have suckers on their ends. They reach forward, stick themselves to the surface of a rock, and pull the sea urchin along. The ones on the animal's back and sides have a mixture of suckers and pinchers on their ends. These keep the animal's spines and back clean by picking off any bits of unwanted debris that happen to land on it.

Some sea urchins use their suckers to put seaweed and stones on their backs. This makes it more difficult for birds such as seagulls to spot them. Seagulls like to eat sea urchins. They carry them into the air, then drop them onto the rocks so that they break open. The bird then eats the inside. Sometimes fish with specially protected mouths will also eat sea urchins.

Migrating Down the Beach

Sea urchins live very low down on the beach. They are left above the water only when the tide goes out a very long way. Sea urchins do not like to be above the water for long, to avoid being spotted by seagulls. Also, they die very easily if they get too hot and dry, or too cold. So most sea urchins migrate toward the water for summer and winter. The farther down the beach they go, the less likely they are to be left above the water when the tide goes out.

In spring, many types migrate back up the beach. At this time of year, there are lots of things on the rocks for them to eat. Also, they are not likely to get too hot or cold.

Crabs and Tide Pool Fish

Crabs use their vicious-looking claws for more than just pinching people's toes. They use them to catch and crack open their food. Crabs are particularly fond of snails. They try to make their homes in a place where there are lots of snails for them to eat. As snails move around throughout the year, so do the crabs. They migrate from one home to another at various times of the year, depending on where most of the snails are.

Some gobies and blennies live in tide pools only during the spring and summer. In fall and winter the water in tide pools often freezes over. To avoid the frozen tide pools, many blennies and gobies migrate down the beach. Here, just like the sea urchins, they live among rocks that are always under water. In winter it never gets as cold in the ocean as it does in tide pools.

The California Sea Lion

If you live in California, you may have been lucky enough to see this magnificent animal in the wild. For most of us, though, the only way of catching a glimpse of the California

sea lion is to go to the zoo.

In the wild, California sea lions have different homes at various times of year. From May to December they live on small islands along the California coast. These small islands are known as "nursery" homes. From May to July, thousands of females haul themselves up onto the beaches to give birth. Sea lions are very heavy animals. It takes a lot of time and effort for each female to drag herself onto the beach. Each female has just one baby. Soon after giving birth she will mate again so

A rock crab from Malindi on the Kenyan coast, about to transfer prey to its mouth. Crabs follow snails, their favorite food.

that another baby is produced the following year.

From July to December the islands are just an enormous nursery. The newborn cubs stay on shore and feed on their mothers' milk. There are thousands of them, all flopping around in the sand and barking loudly at the world. Not all the cubs survive, though. Those that get in the way of fighting males are

sometimes crushed to death. A cub can even be crushed to death by its own mother as she rolls around in the sand.

The baby feeds on its mother's milk until about December. Then it starts to go out to sea with its mother and learns how to catch fish. Eventually the mothers stop producing milk, and the young sea lions have to catch all their own food. Soon after this the mother and cub separate.

In winter the islands are not good homes for sea lions. They need to live in the sea where there are lots of fish for them to eat. So males, females, and young migrate, each by themselves, in search of winter

The California sea lion is the smallest of the five sea lion species. Males migrate north for several hundred miles.

homes in the sea. The males often migrate much farther than the females. Females almost always stay within about 40-60 miles of their home island. The males, however, may migrate several hundred miles to the north along the Canadian coast.

After spending from January to April swimming in the ocean and eating lots of fish, the sea lions are well fed and healthy, with sleek and shiny coats. They are ready to migrate back to their island nursery homes.

24

5 Long-Distance Seasonal Migrations

In the last chapter we looked at a few animals that have different homes at various times of the year. Some, like the sea urchins and tide pool fish, migrate to avoid bad weather. Others, like crabs and the California sea lions, migrate to be in the best place to find food.

None of these animals migrate very long distances. To reach their second homes most of them migrate no more than a few hundred feet. Even the big California sea lion has a winter home that is often less than

The spiny lobster lacks the large claws of other lobsters, but has protective spines and long spiny antennae.

200 miles from its island breeding home. However, not all animals migrate such short distances between one season's home and another. Some have to migrate hundreds or thousands of miles, avoiding all sorts of obstacles.

Lobsters and Prawns

Prawns, large shrimplike fish, and lobsters have strong front claws. They use these claws for catching and crushing their food. Lobsters are much larger than prawns. Some grow as long as 28 inches or more, and are quite fierce.

Many types of prawns and lobsters stay in the same homes all year round. However, the Oriental prawn migrates as far as 400 miles between different summer and winter homes. This prawn lives in the Yellow Sea, which is off the coast of China. The Atlantic prawn lives in the shallow waters off the coast of North America. It often migrates as far as 350 miles between different homes. These migrants often make use of the water currents, like the animals in Chapter 3. This makes the long journey a little less tiring. However, there is a type of lobster that migrates by walking along the ocean bottom! This is the spiny lobster. The spiny lobster lives off the coast of Florida. Every year it walks about

Spiny lobsters of the Florida coast migrate about 60 miles between summer and winter homes. They line up in single file, then actually walk along the ocean floor.

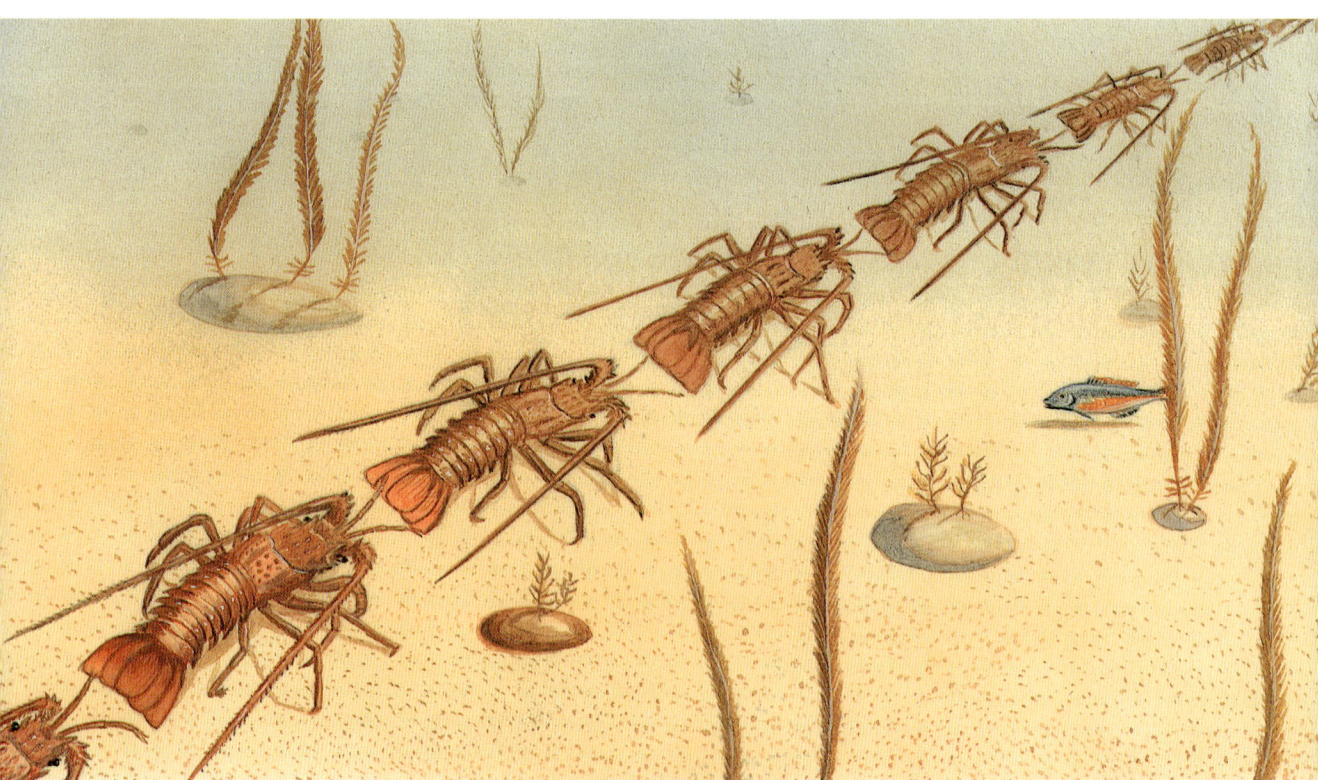

26

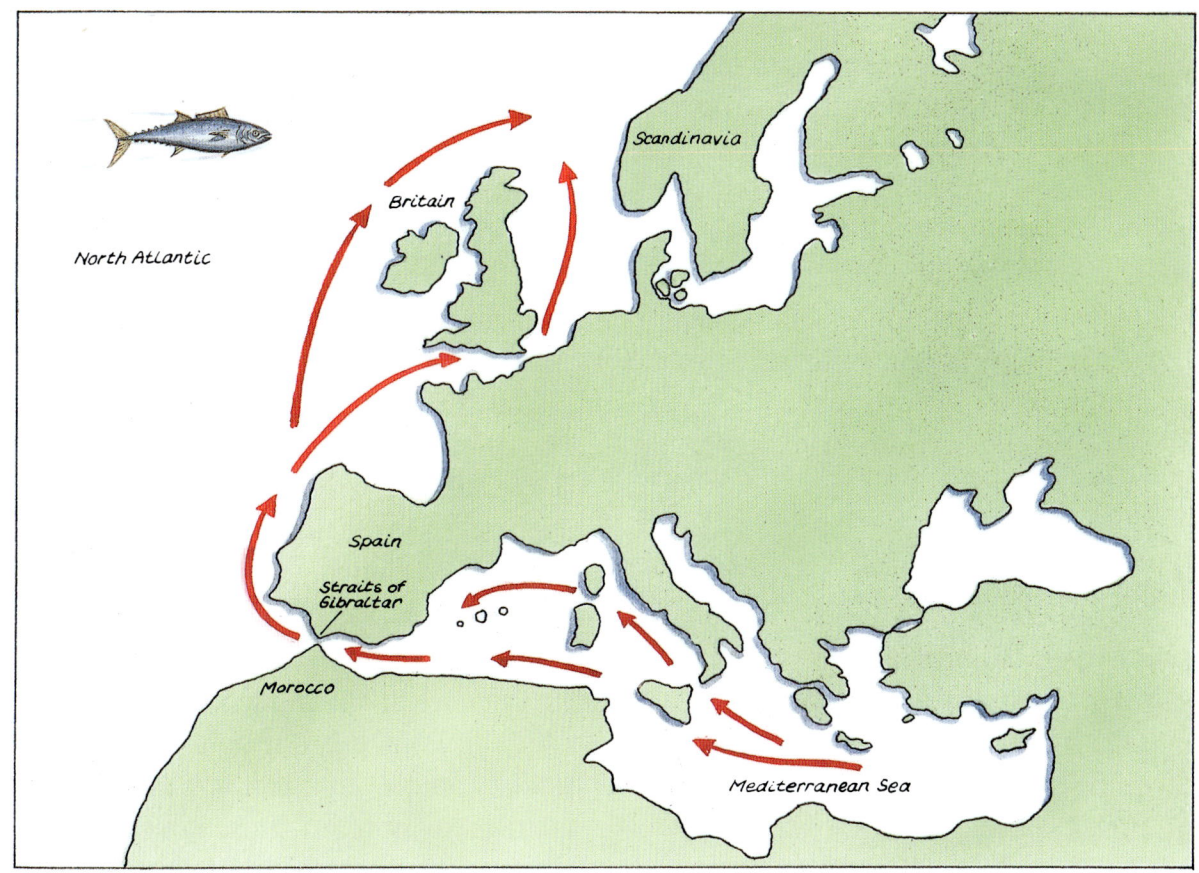

60 miles from its summer home to its winter home.

The migration of the spiny lobster is a remarkable sight. Groups of lobsters get together to form long lines on the ocean bottom. There may be as many as 100 lobsters in one line. Each lobster touches the one in front. This strange procession then marches off down the coast to warmer waters to spend the winter months.

Tuna Fish

This fish is also called the ''bluefin tuna,'' or just the ''tunny.'' The tuna fish is a magnificent animal. It has a beautiful, dark blue back, silvery

Every year the Mediterranean tuna streams through the Straits of Gibraltar. During its 2,500-3,100 miles journey it will travel up to 150 miles per day.

sides, and large gold spots on its fins. The adult is usually about 8 feet long, but some can grow to 13 feet—about twice the height of a fairly tall person.

The tuna feeds on other, smaller fish like sardines, anchovies, mackerel, and herring. It will also eat larger fish like cod. Tuna are found all across the Atlantic Ocean, from the Gulf of Mexico to the Mediterranean Sea. They are also found in the Black Sea, and in parts of the Pacific Ocean. In the

Mediterranean, the tuna first lay eggs in the sea when they are three years old. Most of them then migrate out of the Mediterranean. They pass through the Straits of Gibraltar, the narrow gap between Spain and Africa, in large schools. Some schools contain as many as 10,000 fish. They are heading for their fall homes around Britain and Scandinavia. Sadly, though, many of these magnificent fish never arrive.

Danger from Fishermen

For a migrating tuna fish the greatest danger comes from people. Mediterranean fishermen put out large nets to catch the migrating fish as they pass through the Straits of Gibraltar. The fishermen are nearly always successful. Huge numbers are caught, ending up in cans on the supermarket shelf.

Those tuna that escape the fishermen's nets head north for their fall homes. They travel very fast. Some migrate as far as 3,100 miles in just one month, using the ocean currents to help them on their way. They spend the fall feeding on fish in ocean homes around Britain or Norway. Then, from November on, the tuna start to migrate back to the south. This time they travel at a much slower rate. They will pass again through the Straits of Gibraltar in the spring, and once more fishermen's nets will be waiting there for them.

The Walrus

Most of you are probably familiar with this magnificently ugly animal. It looks like a gigantic seal, except that it has a pair of fabulous tusks, just like the elephant. The walrus lives in the Arctic Circle, near the North Pole.

The North Pole is in the middle of a large sea called the Arctic Ocean. It is so cold at the North Pole that the ocean is covered with a very thick layer of ice that never melts or breaks. Nothing lives there. In winter, the Arctic ice cap spreads all the way from the North Pole to the coasts of Canada, Greenland, and the Soviet Union. In summer, the ice cap shrinks away from these coasts. It leaves a mixture of cold seawater filled with floating blocks of ice called ice "floes." Walruses live at the edge of the Arctic ice cap, and use the ice floes as traveling homes.

Floating Nurseries

Walruses usually feed in the morning. They dive off their ice floes into the freezing water. They can dive down to a depth of 300 feet. Like all types of seals, walruses can hold their breath under water for many minutes. They use their tusks to help them uncover shellfish and other food on the ocean floor. They also use their tusks for fighting.

Young walruses are born on the floating ice floes. Female walruses

Walruses can migrate lazily by hitching a ride on ice floes. The ice floes can drift thousands of miles southward from the frozen Arctic Ocean waters.

give birth every two years in May or June. The young cub feeds on its mother's milk for a whole year. Even when it is old enough to feed itself, it may stay and travel with its mother for another two years or more. The young cub will be six years old before it is able to mate.

The ice floes float on the water. They are blown along by the wind and carried along by water currents. Some ice floes are very large, and whole groups of walruses can sit on them. As the ice floe is carried along, the walruses are carried along on it. How far a walrus migrates each year depends on how far the current takes its ice floe. Ice floes can often drift thousands of miles.

Sometimes ice floes melt or get stuck amid ice or beached on land. Sometimes the ice floats into water so deep that the walruses cannot reach the bottom to feed. If any of these things happen, the walruses swim away and find other ice floes to travel on.

Whales

Whales look like gigantic fish, but they are not fish—they are mammals. They give birth to live young in the water, and feed them with milk from their bodies. Mammals are unable to breathe under water. They have to hold their breath the whole time they are under water, just like you and I. Unlike humans though some whales can hold their breath for up to half an hour! When they come up to the surface to breathe, whales blow huge jets of spray and water into the air from their noses. The whale's nose is just a hole on the top of its head and is called a blowhole.

There are two different groups of whales. One group has big teeth, and so are called toothed whales. They feed on animals such as fish, squid, seals, or even other whales. Examples of this type of whale are the killer whale and the sperm whale. Killer and sperm whales roam the oceans looking for food. They travel in small herds. Some

KILLER WHALE

HUMPBACK WHALE

BLUE WHALE

To show how big whales are, the child and the elephant are drawn in the same scale.

herds migrate thousands of miles each year.

Dolphins and porpoises also belong to this group of mammals. They are really just another, smaller type of toothed whale. Dolphins and porpoises also roam the seas in small herds looking for food. However, they do not migrate as far as the killer and sperm whales do.

The other type of whale is the baleen whale. Baleen whales do not have teeth. They are the biggest of all animals, but feed on very tiny food called krill, and other plankton. When they feed, baleen whales take in big gulps of water. They have special mouths that strain the plankton out of the water. After straining the water out, the plankton is rolled into a big ball which the whale swallows.

It is amazing that whales can grow so large from feeding on such tiny food. A type of baleen whale called the blue whale is the biggest animal that has ever lived on our planet. A fully grown blue whale is about 82 feet long. This is even bigger than the biggest dinosaur that ever lived!

Humpback Whales

The humpback whale is a baleen whale. However, it does not grow as large as the blue whale. When fully grown, this whale is about 42 feet long. The humpback whale is found in oceans all over the world, from the Arctic Ocean all the way down to the Antarctic. Look at the map on pages 6 and 7. Each humpback whale has two homes, one for summer and one for winter.

The humpback makes its summer home in the cold waters near the polar ice. The plankton in these icy waters is very thick. The whales spend the whole summer feeding, and put on a lot of fat. As winter approaches, the ice gradually covers more of the ocean. The whales can

SPERM WHALE

no longer come to the surface to breathe, so they begin the long migration to their winter homes. In small groups, they swim slowly toward the Equator. There is not much plankton in the seas around the Equator. This means that the whales hardly feed at all during this part of their migration.

In the warm, tropical waters near the Equator, the whales give birth. Young whales are called calves. After giving birth, the whales mate again to produce calves that will be born the following year. The calves feed on their mother's milk and grow very rapidly. In spring, the mothers and calves begin the long journey back to the polar feeding grounds

The humpback is one of those whales that feed on plankton, which is plentiful in polar seas. But the whales must return to tropical waters to give birth.

and their summer homes. The males begin their return journey about two weeks later.

Humpback whales make strange and eerie sounds underwater. These sounds are known as the ''song'' of the humpback whale. Perhaps the whales are talking to each other as they travel. The sounds travel a lot farther underwater than they would on land. Some scientists believe humpbacks can talk to each other even when they are hundreds of miles apart.

6 Leaving the Sea

In the last chapter, we looked at a few animals that spend their whole lives on or in the sea. Now we are going to look at a few animals that migrate out of the sea to spend time in other homes. Do you remember the California sea lion? This creature spends part of the year in the sea and the rest of the time on land. In this chapter you will read about another strange animal that has one home on land and another in the sea. This is the sea turtle.

We are also going to look at two types of fish that migrate out of the sea and into the fresh water of rivers and streams. Each year, salmon and eels migrate thousands of miles between their two homes.

Sea Turtles

Sea turtles are just like huge tortoises. Their shells can measure as much as a yard across, and they sometimes weigh as much as 500 pounds. On land, sea turtles have to drag themselves along by their flippers, but in the water they are graceful swimmers. Besides being good swimmers, sea turtles are also able to dive. They can stay under water for long periods, but eventually they have to come up to the surface in order to breathe.

Sea turtles make their homes in the warm waters of tropical seas. Most of the time they stay in the sea and feed on the seaweed that grows along the coasts. They are very long-lived. Some sea turtles live to be over a hundred years old.

Eggs Buried in the Sand

Male sea turtles spend all their lives in the sea. Females are different. Every two or three years, each female has to migrate to a sandy beach in order to lay her eggs. The females stay near the beach for about two months. Then, about every twelve days, in the middle of the night, a very strange spectacle takes place. Hordes of female turtles drag themselves up onto the beach and start digging holes in the sand with their flippers. When the holes are big enough, each female lays about 100 soft, leathery eggs. The eggs are then covered with sand. Sometimes, so many females try to lay their eggs on the same beach that other females come along and dig up eggs laid earlier. These eggs get cold and soon die, or are eaten by birds.

The eggs that manage to stay buried hatch into tiny sea turtles about two months later. By now the mothers are far away, having swum back out to sea soon after laying their eggs. Each tiny turtle is lucky if it survives the first few days of its life. First, the hatchlings have to dig their way up through the sand and onto the beach. Once out in the open they have to run for their lives! Circling above the beach are many birds just waiting for the young turtles to emerge, so that they can eat them.

The amazing thing is that the newly hatched turtles seem to know exactly which way to go to find the water. They scuttle off in the right direction without a moment's hesitation. Even if the ocean is obscured by a sand dune the turtles still know which way to go. Sadly, though, many never make it. Some are carried off and eaten by the birds. Others are suffocated as they dig out of the sand. Even the lucky few that do make it to the sea are not completely out of danger.

In the shallow waters near the coast, large fish, such as sharks, lie in wait for the baby turtles. Sharks are particularly fond of baby turtles. The plucky little turtles swim out to sea as fast as they can. The farther from shore they can get, the safer they will be. However, what happens to those that manage to escape the sharks' jaws is a mystery.

A green turtle. Males spend their entire lives in the sea, but females must visit land in order to lay their eggs.

A baby turtle's migration begins at birth, tunneling up through sand, and then a desperate race down the beach to the sea.

Once in the deeper waters, the baby turtles disappear for about one-and-a-half years. Scientists and divers have taken out boats and spent many days searching for them. None have ever been found. Perhaps they hide in the large mats of floating seaweed that are found in all tropical seas. Or perhaps they are just so tiny that trying to find them is as hopeless as looking for a needle in a haystack!

Where Do the Mothers Go?

After laying their eggs, the mother turtles swim back out to sea. Some of them now have numbers painted on their shells. They have been put there by scientists so that they can recognize the turtles if they see them again. They hope to find out where the mothers go after they leave the nesting beaches.

Most female turtles seem to swim along with the ocean currents. They use the currents to migrate to their coastal feeding homes. Sometimes the currents take the turtles no farther than 20 to 30 miles along the coast from their nesting beaches. At other times the currents take them over a thousand miles across entire oceans. For example, the leatherback turtle crosses the North Atlantic. It travels in the Gulf Stream from the Gulf of Mexico, and shows up mostly on the coasts of Britain and Norway.

The Green Turtle

One type of sea turtle is the green turtle. There is a group of green turtles that lay their eggs on an island in the middle of the Atlantic Ocean. This island is called Ascension Island. These same green turtles have their homes on the coast of Brazil. Every two or three years the females migrate the 1,200 miles to Ascension Island to lay their eggs.

Ascension Island is only five miles

After laying her eggs the turtle returns to the sea. Here a leatherback paddles away through Australia's Great Barrier Reef.

across, and lies right in the middle of the huge Atlantic Ocean. The turtles often have to swim against the current in order to reach it. Swimming against the current is very tiring, even for an animal as large as the turtle. Scientists have no idea how the green turtles from Brazil manage to find such a small island in such a huge ocean.

Scientists also do not know for certain what happens to the babies. Green turtle youngsters do turn up on the coast of Brazil. However, the green turtle nests all over the tropics. Scientists can't be sure whether or not the Ascension Island babies actually return there.

The Salmon

Salmon are beautiful and graceful fish. They are found throughout the northern parts of the Pacific and Atlantic oceans. When they are fully grown, Atlantic salmon are a lovely silvery color. Several different types of salmon live in the Pacific Ocean. When fully grown, some of these types become a bright pink or reddish color. A full-grown salmon is about 28 inches long.

All salmon spend much of their lives in the sea. They migrate with the currents and can sometimes be over 600 miles from the nearest land. They feed on other, smaller fish, but they themselves are the favorite food of seals and sea lions.

When salmon are fully grown they migrate to the coast. Some may have traveled 2,500 miles or so in a big circle with the ocean currents. The Atlantic salmon migrates to the coasts of Europe in the east, and Greenland and North America in the west. Pacific salmon make their way to the coasts of Canada and the

Salmon live in the northern Atlantic and Pacific oceans. When fully grown they migrate to the coasts colored in red.

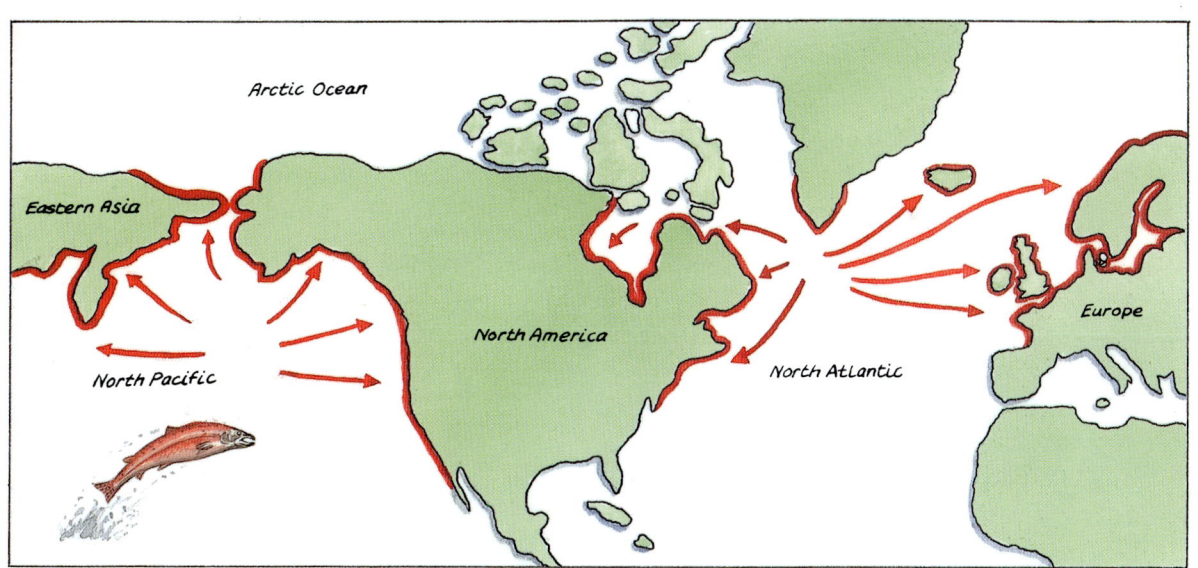

United States and Siberia and Japan in the west.

Once at the coast, the migrants find a river. Lots of salmon crowd together where this river joins the sea. When they are all ready, the fish begin to migrate up the river. They do not stop to feed, and can travel 10 miles each day.

Some salmon swim up very long rivers. In the Soviet Union, they often make their way up rivers as long as 600 miles. They are looking for a special place, a good place to lay their eggs. When salmon lay their eggs it is called "spawning." Usually, the best places to spawn are a long way upstream, in shallow, clear waters.

The migrating salmon are

Salmon choose a river and surge up it, sometimes for up to 600 miles. If they find a waterfall they leap over it.

unstoppable. In addition to swimming through still, quiet lakes, these fish battle their way up fast-flowing streams, struggle against floods, and—most spectacular of all—jump up waterfalls. The only way a salmon can get past a waterfall is by jumping over it. But how does a fish manage to jump out of the water into the air?

When they reach the bottom of a waterfall, the salmon back away a few yards. Then they race back toward the base of the waterfall. They start to swim up toward the surface as they get nearer. At the last

minute they whip their tails very fast. This shoots them out of the water and up into the air.

Salmon can leap over waterfalls that are as high as 11 feet. This is as high as a man with a young child standing on his shoulders. Often it takes the fish several attempts to jump waterfalls as high as this. When they eventually land on top of the waterfall, the salmon swim quickly away before the current carries them back over the edge.

A Feast for the Grizzly Bear

Waterfalls are not the only hazards faced by migrating salmon. In North America, black and grizzly bears catch the salmon in their enormous

In shallow waters the swarming salmon are easy prey for bears, which will often come together to trap them.

paws as they swim past. Sometimes lots of bears gather together and wade in the shallow water. Most dangerous of all, however, are fishermen. For anglers, catching a salmon is a real achievement. They try especially hard to get salmon to bite on their bait.

Eventually, the fish arrive at a good place to spawn. In some long rivers it takes the salmon a whole year to swim from the sea to the spawning site. With her tail, the female digs a hole in the gravel at the bottom of the stream. This is where she lays her eggs. The eggs are fertilized by the nearest male. The female then covers the fertilized eggs with gravel.

By the time the salmon have spawned, they are exhausted. Most are so exhausted that they die without ever returning to the ocean. Some, however, have some strength left and begin the long journey back to salty waters. A year or so later they will be battling their way back upstream to the very same spawning grounds. Once in Scotland, a thirteen-year-old salmon was caught. This unusually old fish had migrated back and forth between the sea and the river spawning grounds no less than five times!

Going Home

The salmon eggs take about three months to hatch into tiny fish. In cold places like Scandinavia and northern Canada, the young salmon may stay in their river homes for as long as eight years. In warmer places, though, like the United States and Britain, they usually stay only about a year. They feed on the worms and insects that live in the river, and slowly get bigger.

When the young salmon are about 4 inches long, they start to migrate downstream toward the ocean. Strangely enough, they are carried

Tiny salmon, still bearing their yolk sacs, swim among unhatched eggs in a stream. One day they will return to the sea.

A fish that can travel over land. Although the Atlantic eel lives most of its life in fresh water, it is born in the sea thousands of miles from its freshwater habitat.

along by the current tail-first! No one quite knows why this is. The salmon migrate very slowly. Often they travel no more than about a mile a day. However, eventually they reach the sea. By then the salmon are fully grown and a beautiful, shining silver color.

Salmon are very clever fish. When the time comes to spawn, each fish manages to find its way back to the very same stream in which it was born. When they are in the sea, how do the salmon know which is their river? Once they have migrated up the river, how do they recognize the stream in which they were born? The answer is that the salmon use their noses! These fish have an excellent sense of smell. Each river and stream has its own particular scent. Salmon remember the scent of the rivers and streams in which they are born. When they migrate back to these same rivers to spawn, the salmon really do follow their noses, all the way home.

The Mystery of the Freshwater Eel

An eel is a long fish that looks a bit like a snake. Some eels always live in the sea, but we are going to look at the freshwater eel. This eel normally lives in lakes and rivers. Sometimes it lives in marshes and swamps. If

the ground is very wet, it even wriggles through the grass and undergrowth, just like a snake. The freshwater eel lives in places around the North Atlantic Ocean: North America, Britain, Scandinavia, France, Belgium, the Netherlands, Germany, for example, and also around the Mediterranean Sea region.

These elvers have already traveled thousands of miles from the Sargasso Sea. Now they swim up an English river.

Although the Atlantic eel lives most of its life in fresh water, it is born in the sea. But nobody knows where. Nobody has ever found an egg of the Atlantic eel. Newly-hatched eels are very flat. They look just like leaves as they float along in the plankton. These tiny flat eels are found in a part of the Atlantic known as the Sargasso Sea. Some people believe that this is where the eels are born, but no one has found an egg to prove it.

Young eels are called elvers. The tiny, flat, leaf-like elvers are gradually carried across the Atlantic Ocean by the currents. It takes them a whole year to migrate from the Sargasso Sea to the coast of North America. It takes them nearly four years, though, to reach the Mediterranean. By the time they arrive at the coast they look a bit more like eels. However, they are almost transparent and are still no more than an inch or so long.

The elvers wriggle their way up rivers and streams. They migrate very slowly, feeding as they go. They are too small to jump over waterfalls like salmon. Instead, they have to crawl up the wet stones beside the waterfall. As they crawl they look like thin, white worms. Eventually they find a suitable home in a lake or river, and by then they have grown into eels.

A Mysterious Disappearance

Eels often stay in their freshwater homes for as long as fifteen years. During this time they grow slowly until they reach a length of about 20 inches. Then they become restless and start to swim downstream

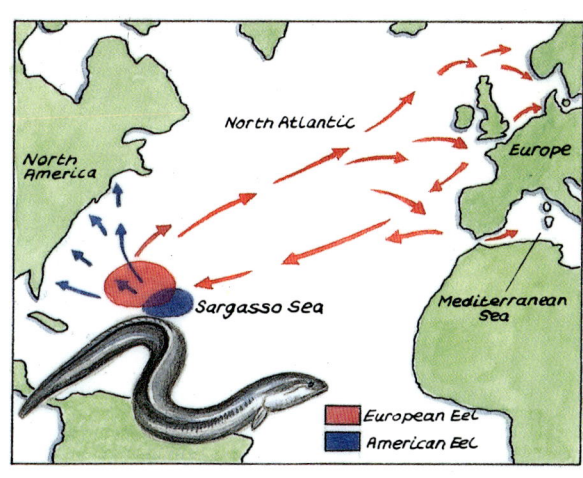

Eels are born in the Sargasso Sea. Some turn left for America, identical ones turn right for Europe. Yet by the time they arrive they can be identified as different species.

toward the sea. As they go, they change color from a yellowish gray to a beautiful silvery color. Also, their eyes begin to grow larger and larger. When the eels reach the sea they swim quickly away from land. Then they start to swim deeper, using their enlarged eyes to help them see in the dark waters. They swim deeper, and deeper, and deeper... then they disappear.

Scientists have tried to follow the eels at sea to find out where they go. They have hired big boats with all kinds of expensive equipment to try and track them. So far, the eels have always escaped their pursuers. Nobody knows what happens to the eels or where they go. Perhaps they go back to the Sargasso Sea, lay their eggs, and die. Or perhaps they live for many more years deep at the bottom of the Atlantic Ocean. Nobody knows the answer yet.

Glossary

Antarctic The whole area of the globe lying to the south of 66 1/2 degrees south latitude.

current A steady flow of wind or water that moves faster than the surrounding wind or water.

egg The form of life in which many creatures, including fish and reptiles, first appear from their mothers' bodies. They are usually produced in vast numbers, and drift in the water until they hatch.

Equator The (imaginary) line around the center of the globe separating the northern and southern hemispheres. Most of the Earth's hottest regions are at sea level on the Equator. There is no winter or summer.

fertilize To make eggs capable of growing and developing by joining them with male sperm.

fresh water Water that is not salty, as it is in the ocean.

Gulf Stream A warm current that flows from the Gulf of Mexico northeastward to northwest Europe.

habitat The type of place where a particular plant or animal lives naturally.

herd A number of wandering mammals living together as a group.

home The habitat of those sea creatures that are not wanderers.

ice cap The thick mass of ice that permanently covers the polar regions.

mammal All creatures whose young feed on milk from the mother's body.

mating A female animal joining with a male animal to produce eggs or live young.

migrant/migrate/migration The habit of moving from one habitat to another (usually in search of food) is called *migration*. An animal that *migrates* is a *migrant*.

north The direction a compass needle points. Most maps are drawn so that the northernmost part is at the top.

North Pole The northernmost point of the Earth. It is surrounded by ocean covered with permanent ice.

plankton Tiny creatures, some too small to be seen, that drift on the surface of the sea, and upon which other creatures feed.

polar Polar regions are the regions around the North and South Poles where it is always icy and very cold.

Sargasso Sea An area of the North Atlantic (see map on page 43) covered with floating brown vegetation.

school A large number of fish of the same kind swimming together.

south The direction opposite to north.

spawn To deposit large numbers of eggs in water, usually by fish.

tide The twice daily rise and fall of the sea on a shore. It is caused by the gravitational pull of the sun and moon.

tropics An area around the center of the Earth reaching 23 1/2 degrees on either side of the Equator. Within this band, about 3,400 miles wide, the climate is very hot.

More Books to Read

Children's books containing some information on migration

Allan, Doug *The Seal on the Rocks* Gareth Stevens 1988

Bunting, Eve *Sea World of Sharks* Harcourt Brace Jovanovich 1984

Bunting, Eve *Sea World of Whales* Harcourt Brace Jovanovich 1987

Green, Carl R. & Sanford, William R. *The Bottlenose Dolphin* Crestwood House 1987

Green, Carl & Sanford, William R. *The Walrus* Crestwood House 1986

Headstrom, Richard *Adventures with Freshwater Animals* Dover Publications 1983

Johnson, Sylvia A. *Crabs* Lerner Publications 1982

Lye, Keith *Coasts* Silver Burdett Press 1988

Patent, Dorothy H. *Dolphins and Porpoises* Holiday House 1987

Penny, Malcolm *Animal Migration* Franklin Watts 1987

Robinson, W. Wright *Incredible Facts about the Ocean: The Restless Blue Salt Water* Dillon Press 1986

Seddon, Tony *Animal Movement* Facts on File 1988

Sharp, David *Animals from the Rivers and Oceans* Salem House Publishers 1987

Sibbald, Jean H. *Sea Mammals: The Warm-Blooded Ocean Explorers* Dillon Press 1988

Wildlife Education, Ltd. *Seals and Sea Lions* Wildlife Education 1985

Picture Sources

Index

© Copyright 1991 Young Library Ltd.
Corsham, Wiltshire, England